Sayings and their Meanings

Don't Judge a Book by its Cover

R. J. Clarke

Contents

Introduction

Sayings are also known as proverbs, which are short phrases that express ideas, thoughts and emotions.

Furthermore, they will often emphasize a truthful point by giving useful advice, a warning or the right attitude to solve a problem.

You will find sayings in ancient literature, religious texts and from many different cultures.

The reason that they have survived for so long is because people have been passing them on to one another for generations. It also helps that they tend to be short and easy to remember.

What makes sayings so great is that their meaning is understood by reading between the lines.

Animals

Even a worm will turn
This means - Everybody has a point in which they will rise in rebellion and fight. Even a worm will defend itself if it is being attacked

When the cat's away, the mice will play
This means - When somebody in authority is not around, then mischief and misbehaving will follow

Birds of a feather flock together
This means - People that have a lot of similarities will tend to stay together

A leopard cannot change its spots
This means - An unpleasant person will not change because it is in their nature to behave like that

There is plenty more fish in the sea
This means - There are plenty of other people to form a relationship with

The last straw that broke the camel's back
This means - The final thing that once added to a series of minor bad things, will lead to a major bad situation. People may also say, "That's the last straw" meaning that they can't take anymore

You can't teach an old dog new tricks
This means - It is impossible to change somebody's habits because the older a person becomes, the less willing they are to change their way of doing things

A bird in the hand is worth two in the bush
This means - It is better to be complacent and keep hold of what you've got rather than to risk chasing after or pursuing something better

You can lead a horse to water but you can't make it drink
This means - You can give somebody an opportunity to do something but you can't make them do something that they are unwilling to do

Dog eat dog
This means - A situation in which the strongest or most determined person will win in a ruthless competition

Talk the hind legs off a donkey
This means - Someone that doesn't stop talking

The early bird catches the worm
This means - It is better to go out and do something before someone else does it before you

The second mouse gets the cheese
This means - It is better to let somebody else go first

There is more than one way to skin a cat
This means - You can achieve the same goal in many ways

Don't put the cart in front of the horse
This means - You should do things in the correct order

Attitudes

Live and let live
This means - We should live our own lives and let others live their lives

A problem shared is a problem halved
This means - Problems are solved much easier if they are discussed with other people

One good turn deserves another
This means - If somebody helps you, then you should help them

Where there's a will, there's a way
This means - If somebody has a desire and determination to do something, then they'll find a method of doing it

Share and share alike
This means - If you share, then other people will share too

Easy come, easy go
This means - If something is easily obtained, it is just as easily lost

Kindness begets kindness
This means - If you are kind to other people, they will be kind to you

If you can't beat them, join them
This means - If you can't succeed in changing your opponent's ideas, then you should change your ideas instead

Fool me once, shame on you. Fool me twice, shame on me
This means - You shouldn't make the same mistake twice

He who hesitates is lost
This means - In a situation, you should make a decision quickly because if you wait to think about it, the opportunity will be lost

If you're not part of the solution, you're part of the problem
This means - If you're not helping to sort a problem, you start becoming a hindrance

Bigger is better
This means - Something that is larger in size is considered better than a smaller size

Familiarity breeds contempt
This means - The people you come to know well will know your faults and you may find yourself scorning them

If at first you do not succeed, try, try again
This means - If you are persistent, you can achieve your goal in life

A miss is as good as a mile
This means - Even if you have lost by a small amount, it is still the same as losing by a large amount

Nothing ventured, nothing gained
This means - You have to try to do something if you want to achieve it

Don't put off for tomorrow what you can do today
This means - You should not delay doing something unnecessarily

Family and Friends

Blood is thicker than water
This means - The bonds between family relationships are greater than other relationships

A friend to all is a friend to none
This means - If somebody is friends with everyone then it becomes impossible to make anyone feel special

It takes two to tango
This means - It takes two people to have sexual intercourse, so responsibilities should be shared equally

A friend in need is a friend indeed
This means - Someone that helps you in a time of trouble is considered as a real friend

Like father, like son
This means - A child that acts or behaves similar to his father. The saying can also be rephrased as 'like mother, like daughter'

A good man is hard to find
This means - A woman may say this if she's finding it difficult to find a suitable man to form a relationship with

Two is company, three is a crowd
This means - A third person is seen as an unwelcome person

Keep your friends close and your enemies closer
This means - You'll be safer if you're closer to your enemies than to your friends because it is better to know more about your enemies

Food and Drink

You can't make an omelette without breaking any eggs
This means - There will be times when you will have to sacrifice something to achieve something else

An apple a day keeps the doctor away
This means - The nutrition from apples will help to keep you healthy

The apple doesn't fall far from the tree
This means - The child is going to behave similar to its parents

A rotten apple spoils the barrel
This means - One bad person can have a negative influence on a group of people

You are what you eat
This means - The food that you consume will affect your health and appearance

Variety is the spice of life
This means - Changes in somebody's daily routine is good because it makes their life more interesting, in the sense as adding spices to plain food

Eat to live, but do not live to eat
This means - We should not live our lives just focusing on enjoying food because we are made to do so much more

Water, water everywhere but not a drop to drink
This means - The ocean is full of water but its high salt content makes it harmful to drink

One man's meat is another man's poison
This means - Each man has his own likes and dislikes regarding food

Your eyes are bigger than your belly
This means - You overestimate what you are capable of eating

Life is like a box of chocolate, you never know what you'll get
This means - The events in your life are unexpected and you won't be able to choose everything that happens in it

You can't have your cake and eat it
This means - You must make a compromise because you can't have both things

A watched pot never boils
This means - If you constantly watch over something it feels like it takes a much longer time

Too many cooks spoil the broth
This means - If too many people are trying to do the same thing together, it won't be done properly

Don't bite off more than you can chew
This means - You shouldn't take on more responsibility if you can't manage it

It's not my cup of tea
This means - Something that you wouldn't choose to have for yourself

If you want breakfast in bed, sleep in the kitchen
This means - A humorous saying, implying that if somebody wants something, they'll have to do it themselves

The bread always falls buttered side down
This means - A pessimistic outlook on a situation

Don't bite the hand that feeds you
This means - You shouldn't hurt the person that pays or cares for you

Out of the frying pan and into the fire
This means - When a bad situation turns into a worse situation

It's no use crying over spilt milk
This means - You shouldn't worry over something that can't be undone

Man doesn't live on bread alone
This means - People need to meet their physical needs as well as their psychological needs

The proof of the pudding is in the eating
This means - You have to try something before you can make a judgement on it

Honey catches more flies than vinegar
This means - More cooperation is gained from others by being nice

Give a man a fish and you feed him for a day; teach a man how to fish and you feed him for a lifetime

This means - Instead of giving something to someone, it would be wiser to teach them how to help themselves

Health and Safety

Better safe than sorry
This means - It is better to be cautious and careful rather than doing anything that could be regretted later on

Prevention is better than cure
This means - It is easier and better to prevent something from happening than to try to deal with the consequences of it

Rubbing salt into the wound
This means - Making a situation even worse

If you don't use it, you lose it
This means - You have to use something regularly to be able to keep it. For instance, if you don't use your mind or legs, you'll start to lose those abilities

Coughs and sneezes spread diseases
This means - Germs can be spread when coughing and sneezing so it is important to catch them in a tissue and throw them away

Laughter is the best medicine
This means - Laughing is good for your health and well-being

Early to bed and early to rise makes a man healthy, wealthy and wise
This means - It's good for us to sleep early and wake up early

Home

There is no place like home
This means - Somebody that feels that home is the best place in the world

When one door shuts, another opens
This means - An opportunity will follow after a failure.

If you can't stand the heat, get out of the kitchen.
This means - If you are under too much pressure from a situation, you should get out of the situation as soon as possible

Charity begins at home
This means - A person's first responsibility is to help and care for their own family before helping others

Home is where the heart is
This means - You feel that the most comfortable place is at home

A house divided against itself cannot stand
This means - Arguments and disagreements can break the family up

An Englishman's home is his castle
This means - The home of an English man is where he can feel safe and enjoy doing what he wants in privacy

Law and Justice

Honesty is the best policy
This means - It is much better to be truthful than dishonest

Rules are made to be broken
This means - We shouldn't obey every rule, instead we should think for ourselves

The end justifies the means
This means - If somebody's objective is good, then it doesn't matter if they have to do something bad to achieve it

It takes a thief to catch a thief
This means - Someone has to think and act like a thief. Can be applied to anything, such as a dishonest person would be able to find another dishonest person if they wanted to

Justice delayed is justice denied
This means - If somebody is in court, they should have a speedy trial period

There is no honour amongst thieves
This means - There is no trust between dishonest people

Love

All is fair in love and war
This means - What happens in love and war can often be excuse because they often defy reason

Absence makes the heart grow fonder
This means - Time spent apart from two people that love each other, will make their love grow stronger

Love is blind
This means - A person that is in love will not be able to see the faults with the person they are in love with

The way to a man's heart is through his stomach
This means - Some women have found that if a man is fed well with delicious food, she is more likely to win his heart and to fall in love

To worship the ground somebody walks on
This means - In love with somebody

Beauty is only skin deep
This means - A person's character is valued above their appearance

Beauty is in the eye of the beholder
This means - Each person's perception of what is beauty is different to each other

Marry in haste, repent at leisure
This means - If you get married too quickly, you may spend a long time regretting it

It's better to have loved and lost than to have never loved at all
This means - It is better to have experienced love than to never know what love feels like

Love makes the world go round
This means - When people are considerate and respectful to each other, it makes the world a better place to live

Mind

Great minds think alike
This means - Intelligent people tend to think the same. This saying is said jokingly if two people think of the same thing at the same time

Knowledge is power
This means - By having intelligence, facts and information you will be better able to influence things

Mind over matter
This means - The ability of your mind can overcome physical obstacles

Learn to walk before you can run
This means - Patience is needed so that you progress gradually to what you want to achieve

Ignorance is bliss
This means - If you don't know something then it can't cause any sadness

Forgive and forget
This means - To not dwell on a past event

Be careful what you wish for, you just might get it
This means - You shouldn't wish for something that you would regret if it came true, such as 'I wish you'd drop dead'

You are never too old to learn
This means - People can learn things at any age

Money

Money doesn't grow on trees
This means - Money shouldn't be wasted because it isn't easy to get

Money is the root of all evil
This means - The love of money is the main cause of the problems that lead to immorality and wickedness

Money makes money
This means - If you have money, it can be used to earn more money through investments

Time is money
This means - Time is considered valuable

Health is better than wealth
This means - It is much better to be healthy than to have lots of money

Don't put all your eggs in one basket
This means - It is better to spread your risks than to rely on a single plan of action. For example, you shouldn't place all your money in one investment

You can't take it with you when you die
This means - The money and material things accumulated in your life aren't really as important as you think

Robbing Peter to pay Paul
This means - Not a very sensible way of managing money or problems

Money isn't everything
This means - There are more important things in life than money

Penny wise, pound foolish
This means - Somebody that is careful with managing small amounts of money, but careless with managing their larger finances

A fool and his money will easily be parted
This means - If somebody spends their money foolishly, they will soon run out of money

Money talks
This means - Having money will give you greater influence in getting what you want

Every man has his price
This means - All men can be bribed if the price is right

The best things in life are free
This means - Things like friendship, love and happiness are things that you don't have to pay for and are considered the best things in people's lives

Where there's muck, there's brass
This means - Fortunes can be earned by doing what is considered a dirty job

If you pay peanuts, you get monkeys
This means - An employer that pays their staff low wages should expect to get bad staff

A bad penny always turns up
This means - Something or someone that you dislike that has a habit of returning

Winning is earning. Losing is learning
This means - You gain financially if you win, but if you don't win you should learn why you didn't so you'll win next time

Born with a silver spoon in his/her mouth
This means - A person that is born into a wealthy family

A penny saved is a penny earned
This means - By being cautious with your money, you'll be able to save yourself money

If you buy cheaply, you pay dearly
This means - If you don't spend a lot of money then you will get low quality product

Rags to rags in three generations
This means - The family's first generation makes a lot of money (rags to riches), the second generation maintains the money, whilst the third generation loses the money

Fortunes knocks on everyone's door once
This means - An opportunity for success will arrive to everyone at some point in their lifetime

If it sounds too good to be true, then it probably is
This means - If somebody offers you something that seems really good for no reason that could benefit the other person, you should be very wary

Behind every successful man is a woman
This means - Many men owe their successful achievements to the help given from their partner

There are two sides to every coin
This means - There are always two sides of view in a dispute.

One man's trash is another man's treasure
This means - One man may see something as invaluable, whilst another man may see the same thing as valuable

It pays to pay attention
This means - People that are aware of what is happening in the past, present and future, will get rewarded.

Strike while the iron is hot
This means - We should seize the opportunity straight away before it's too late

Put your money where your mouth is
This means - If you're so confident that you are speaking the truth, would you bet your money on it

Objects

Don't judge a book by its cover
This means - The appearance of someone or something can be deceptive

A chain is no stronger than its weakest link
This means - The strength of a group of people is dependent on each person in it

The squeaking wheel gets the grease
This means - A person that makes a fuss about something will be the one that gets the attention

How long is a piece of string?
This means - The length of something can be anything that you want it to be

The ball is in your court
This means - The decision is up to the other person to make

Don't cross a bridge until you've come to it
This means - You shouldn't worry about something that hasn't happened yet

Been there, done that, got the t-shirt
This means - You're familiar with a situation or you've already been or done something that has been mentioned

Don't look a gift horse in the mouth
This means - If something has been given to you, you shouldn't complain about it

See a pin/penny and pick it up, all the day you'll have good luck
This means - You will have good luck if you pick it up. In another similar saying 'if you see a pin and let it lay, bad luck you'll have all the day' means you'll get bad luck if you don't pick it up

A picture is worth a thousand words
This means - An image can provide someone with a lot of information

Good things come in small packages
This means - A small package can hold valuable things. For example, an engagement ring in a box

All that glitters is not gold
This means - Things aren't as valuable as they appear to be

People and Body Parts

You scratch my back and I'll scratch yours
This means - If you are willing to help me, then I'll help you

You have eyes on the back of your head
This means - You have the ability to be aware of everything around you

Burn the candle at both ends
This means - People that are living very busy lifestyles with very little rest

No man is an island
This means - Nobody lives in isolation because everybody needs to have other people in their lives

In one ear and out the other
This means - Somebody has said something to you, but you were not listening to them

Don't cut off your nose to spite your face
This means - You shouldn't deliberately do something that is nasty and annoying to someone if it is going to hurt you too

Two heads are better than one
This means - Two people will be more likely to solve a problem than one person

Caught red handed
This means - Somebody that has done something wrong and been found with the evidence so that they can't deny they did it

Boys will be boys
This means - Something that is said to excuse bad behaviour in boys and men

An eye for an eye
This means - A punishment that should be equal to the crime committed

One hand washes the other
This means - Helping someone will result in them helping you

United we stand, divided we fall
This means - By working together, we'll be successful but if we aren't working together, we'll fail

If God had wanted man to fly, he would have given him wings
This means - There are things that we are just not supposed to do

Stranger danger
This means - Beware of people that you do not know

It's like getting blood out of a stone
This means - It's really difficult to get an answer from somebody

The more the merrier
This means - More people will add to the excitement of the event

A man is known by the company he keeps
This means - A person is believed to be similar to the people they spend their time with

My body is my temple
This means - Your body is something that you look after, especially regarding the things you consume

Plants

Great oaks grow from little acorns
This means - Great and wonderful things start from small and modest things and with time will flourish into something great

A rose by any other name would smell just as sweet
This means - The name given to something is not important; it's what it is that is important

A big tree attracts the woodman's axe
This means - The more famous a person is, the more criticism they are likely to receive

Rude

He who denied it, supplied it
This means - If somebody denies passing wind, then they must be the one that passed it

He who smelt it, dealt it
This means - The first person to claim that they smelled that wind has been passed is sometimes the culprit, because they are trying to look like the innocent one

Loud and proud
This means - Somebody that feels no shame in passing wind in a noisily manner

Better out than in
This means - It is better to burp or pass wind than to keep it inside your body

If it's yellow, let it mellow, if it's brown flush it down
This means - When going to the toilet, flushing is not done after doing a wee, but flushing is done after doing a poo

Now the shit has really hit the fan
This means - When a situation, usually a scandal has been made public and its consequences are very messy and chaotic

Senses and Emotions

Say something nice or say nothing at all
This means - You should only say nice things to someone and avoid saying nasty things

Do as I say, not as I do
This means - You should follow someone's vocal instructions rather than what they are doing

It's not over until the fat lady sings
This means - You shouldn't assume the outcome of an event until its finished

Actions speak louder than words
This means - The things that a person does are better than what they say they will do

In the kingdom of the blind, the one-eyed man is king
This means - A person that has a limited ability to do something will be able to do something better than somebody that has even less of an ability to do something

Laugh and the world laughs with you, cry and you cry alone.
This means - If somebody is happy and cheerful, people like to be around you, sharing the joy.
However, if you are upset, other people don't want to feel upset so won't want to be around

Out of sight, out of mind
This means - Things that we do not see, we don't think about

The blind leading the blind
This means - Someone that is helping or advising people but has the same limited information as them

What you see is what you get
This means - There is just what is real and nothing hidden

Losers weepers, finders keepers
This means - If something has been lost, the owner will weep, whilst the person that finds it will get to keep it

No pain, no gain
This means - If you are trying to achieve something, you can expect to push yourself because it will be difficult

Practice what you preach
This means - Follow your own advice that you give to others

Someone's bark is worse than their bite
This means - Somebody that can say nasty things but wouldn't be able to physically harm someone much

Cold hands, warm heart
This means - Inside, somebody can have compassion even if they appear to be unapproachable

Look before you leap
This means - You should think before you act

He who laughs last, laughs best
This means - The person who has the final success, has the most to laugh about

Misery loves company
This means - Unhappy people enjoy making other people unhappy

Hindsight is better than foresight
This means - If something has happened to you in the past, you will be more likely to understand it better than if it didn't happen

Many a true word spoken in jest
This means - Sometimes a joke contains both wisdom and truth

It's like looking for a needle in a haystack
This means - Something that seems impossible to find

Time

A stitch in time saves nine
This means - It's better to sort out a small problem straight away before it becomes more difficult to sort out

Time flies when you're having fun
This means - When you are enjoying yourself, time seems to go quickly

There's no time like the present
This means - The present moment is the best

Patience is a virtue
This means - Being patient is a good thing

The truth will out
This means - The truth will be discovered by somebody eventually

Third time lucky
This means - Your luck will improve the third time around

There is no fool like an old fool
This means - An older person is expected to behave and to have matured by now

You are only as old as you feel
This means - Somebody may be old, but inside they can feel any age

Life begins at forty

This means - You can start to enjoy your life at the age of forty because you don't have so many worries at this age

Better late than never

This means - It is better to make an effort even if it is late than to give up

First come, first served

This means - The person that has waited in line first, is the first to be attended to

All good things come to those that wait

This means - Patience will be rewarded with good things

No news is good news

This means - By not hearing any news it can be assumed that the news is good because any bad news would have travelled quickly

Bad news travels fast

This means - Bad news about something or someone is quickly known by other people

Travel

What goes around comes around
This means - If somebody does or says something bad, it will come back on themselves later on

What goes up must come down
This means - Things that can be really good, won't always stay that way

When in Rome, do as the Romans do
This means - If you are visiting a foreign country, you should behave in a similar way to the people living there

Rome was not built in a day
This means - To do a job properly it will take time so results shouldn't be expected immediately

If you wish to criticise someone, first walk a mile in their shoes. Then when you do criticise you are a mile away and have their shoes
This means - You should try to think what it is like for the person you are criticising before giving criticism

The first step is the hardest
This means - The hardest part of something is starting it

Violence and Insults

Revenge is a dish best served cold
This means - It is more satisfying to take your revenge at a later time, rather than immediately

Two wrongs don't make a right
This means - It is wrong for somebody to harm or offend you, but it is also wrong to harm or offend them back

The pen is mightier than the sword
This means - Words and communication are more effective than violence and aggression

It takes one to know one
This means - Someone that has criticised you has the same faults as you. For instance, if they call you an idiot, they must also be an idiot

Sticks and stones will break my bones, but words will never hurt me
This means - Nasty remarks and comments won't be able to hurt you, but a physical attack will

What doesn't kill you can only make you stronger
This means - You will become fitter and stronger if you put your body under a bit of pressure because your body will adapt

People that live in glass houses shouldn't throw stones
This means - You shouldn't criticise someone over their faults when you share the same or similar faults.

He that lives by the sword shall die by the sword
This means - If you are violent to other people, then you should expect to be treated violently back

He who runs away, lives to fight another day
This means - You don't have to be a coward by avoiding a difficult situation

The bigger they are, the harder they fall
This means - The more successful a person is, the more they have to lose

So you can talk the talk, but can you walk the walk
This means - When somebody questions your ability to back up your boastful talking with physical action

It's better to die on one's feet than to live on one's knees
This means - It's better to live your life having freedom to control your own life than to live at the mercy of others

The best defence is a good offence
This means - If you are offensive and take out your opponent, then you will not need a defense

Waste

Waste not want not
This means - If nothing is wasted, then you'll have the resources for what you need, when it is needed

Haste makes waste
This means - If something is done in a hurry, it won't be made well and may need making again, creating more waste

Garbage in, garbage out
This means - You get out of things what you put into them

The solution to pollution is dilution
This means - To solve the problem of pollution, you shouldn't concentrate it, you should spread it out so that it is at harmless levels

Weather and Environment

Every cloud has a silver lining
This means - Even in an unpleasant situation, there is still something positive

It's raining cats and dogs
This means - It's raining heavily

Make hay while the sun shines
This means - Make the most of an opportunity whilst it is still available

Red sky at night, shepherd's delight; red sky in the morning, shepherd's warning
This means - You will have rain in the morning because the weather moves in from the west, so you should prepare yourself. This saying was also used by sailors

Lightning never strikes in the same place twice
This means - It is unusual for the situation to happen again

No smoke without fire
This means - A rumour that has some truth in it

Still waters run deep
This means - People that appear quiet and calm on the outside are wise and have strong personalities on the inside

Don't make a mountain out of a molehill
This means - You shouldn't exaggerate or make a big issue of something of minor importance

Between a rock and a hard place
This means - You are in a difficult situation

The sky is the limit
This means - There is no limit to what can be achieved

The grass is always greener on the other side
This means - You'll always see and want something else that you can't get

A rolling stone gathers no moss
This means - Someone that moves often will not be able to settle and make friends or gain possessions easily

Men are from Mars and Women are from Venus
This means - Men and women are very different from each other

It never rains, but it pours
This means - Bad events that tend to come in clusters

Work

The devil makes work for idle hands
This means - If someone is not busy working because of their idleness, they will become tempted to cause mischief

Jack of all trades, master of none
This means - Somebody that claims to be good at lots of different trades are probably not very good at any of them

A bad workman always blames his tools
This means - A poorly skilled person that blames their materials or tools rather than blaming themselves

If you snooze you lose
This means - If you don't act quickly enough, you won't be rewarded

Many hands make light work
This means - The workload is easier if it is shared between many people

A woman's work is never done
This means - Typically said by a woman, to suggest that they seem to be working all the time

All work and no play makes Jack a dull boy
This means - Everyone needs time to relax and enjoy themselves

The customer is always right
This means - Businesses usually agree that a customer is right because they don't want to make the customer feel stupid even if they did make a mistake

Beggars can't be choosers
This means - If you are in need of something, you should be grateful for what you are given rather than being fussy or demanding

Never do things by halves
This means - You should not do an incomplete job; you should finish it off completely before starting another job

You don't keep a dog and bark yourself
This means - If you are paying somebody to do a job, you shouldn't be doing it for them

If you fake it, you can make it
This means - By pretending to have or be something you aren't, you can achieve success

If you want something done right, do it yourself
This means - If paying other people to do a job, they won't care so much about doing a job properly

Practice makes perfect
This means - Doing the same thing repeatedly will make you an expert

Do not have too many irons in the fire
This means - If you try to do too many tasks at once, you won't be able to do any tasks properly

If it ain't broke, don't fix it
This means - Don't try to repair something that isn't damaged

When the going gets tough, the tough get going
This means - Physically or mentally strong people will worker harder to resolve a problem when a situation has become more difficult

If a job worth doing is a job, it is worth doing well
This means - You should do a job to the best of your ability

Reap what you sow
This means - You'll have to accept the consequences of your earlier actions

Slow and steady wins the race
This means - If you work at a slow but constant rate, you will be able to do more work than someone that works faster but needs to take more rests

Too many chiefs, not enough Indians
This means - There are too many people giving orders

If you're in a hole, stop digging
This means - If you are in trouble, you should try to get out of it as soon as possible, otherwise you will be making it harder or worse to get out of trouble

Anti-proverbs

Anti-proverbs, are sayings that have been changed slightly to create a humorous effect that transforms its meaning.

To be effective, the sayings should be popular, funny and contain good content. They are popular in advertisements because of their wit and ease to remember.

Here are some examples of anti-proverbs:

An onion a day, keeps your friends away

Absence makes the heart go wander

Where there's a will, there's a lawsuit

Sayings with Contradictions

Sayings are often used as a guidance to how we should live our lives. However, the problem is that there are sayings that contradict each other. These contradictions are found in all cultures and even in the Bible, which has played a prominent role in distributing sayings.

Here are some examples of contradictions:

The pen is mightier than the sword
This saying is contradicted by - Actions speak louder than words

Opposites attract
This saying is contradicted by - Birds of a feather flock together

Look before you leap
This saying is contradicted by - He who hesitates is lost

The early bird catches the worm
This saying is contradicted by - The second mouse eats the cheese

Made in the USA
Middletown, DE
31 July 2019